Rhythm Encyclopedia

by

Bill Woods

Online Audio

To Access the Online Audio Recording Go to:
www.melbay.com/30559MEB

6,561 Different Rhythms
for
Drum Set
Cajon
Conga
and
Djembe

Important! Read This First!

This is NOT an instruction book. I assume you already know how to play your instrument before you use this book.

This book contains 6,561 different rhythms. By interpreting the notation in different ways, these rhythms can be played on drum set, cajon, conga, and djembe.

The notation for these exercises uses three symbols: a normal eighth note with the head on the bottom line of the staff (*symbol 1*), a normal eighth note with the head on the middle line of the staff (*symbol 2*), and an eighth note with a modified head with the head on the third space of the staff (*symbol 3*).

For standard drum set playing, where the right hand keeps a steady eighth note pattern on the high hat while the left hand plays the snare drum and the foot plays the bass drum, *symbol 1* indicates simultaneous bass drum and high hat strikes, *symbol 2* indicates simultaneous snare drum and high hat strikes, and *symbol 3* indicates a high hat strike with no snare or bass drum.

For linear drumming on the drum set, where only one instrument at a time is played, *symbol 1* indicates a bass drum strike, *symbol 2* indicates a snare drum strike, and *symbol 3* indicates a high hat strike.

For all other drums, *symbol 1* indicates a bass tone, *symbol 2* indicates an open tone, and *symbol 3* indicates either a rest or a touch.

These exercises should provide you with many hours of practice material and get you used to playing many different stick or hand patterns. I hope you find them enjoyable and useful.

If you plan on using the audio files for this book, please go to the last page of the book (page 140) for some important information on how the audio files are arranged.

1
2
3
4
5
6
7
8
9
10
11
12
13
14
15
16
17
18
19
20
21
22
23
24
25
26
27
28
29
30
31
32
33
34
35
36
37
38
39
40
41
42
43
44
45
46
47
48

The Rhythms on this page are on **track 2** of the audio file.

The rhythms on this page are on **track 3** of the audio file

The rhythms on this page are on **track 4** of the audio file

193
194
195
196
197
198
199
200
201
202
203
204
205
206
207
208
209
210
211
212
213
214
215
216
217
218
219
220
221
222
223
224
225
226
227
228
229
230
231
232
233
234
235
236
237
238
239
240

The rhythms on this page are on **track 6** of the audio file

289
290
291
292
293
294
295
296
297
298
299
300
301
302
303
304
305
306
307
308
309
310
311
312
313
314
315
316
317
318
319
320
321
322
323
324
325
326
327
328
329
330
331
332
333
334
335
336

The rhythms on this page are on **track 8** of the audio file

385
386
387
388
389
390
391
392
393
394
395
396
397
398
399
400
401
402
403
404
405
406
407
408
409
410
411
412
413
414
415
416
417
418
419
420
421
422
423
424
425
426
427
428
429
430
431
432

433
434
435
436
437
438
439
440
441
442
443
444
445
446
447
448
449
450
451
452
453
454
455
456
457
458
459
460
461
462
463
464
465
466
467
468
469
470
471
472
473
474
475
476
477
478
479
480

481
482
483
484
485
486
487
488
489
490
491
492
493
494
495
496
497
498
499
500
501
502
503
504
505
506
507
508
509
510
511
512
513
514
515
516
517
518
519
520
521
522
523
524
525
526
527
528

The rhythms on this page are on **track 12** of the audio file

The rhythms on this page are on **track 13** of the audio file

625
626
627
628
629
630
631
632
633
634
635
636
637
638
639
640
641
642
643
644
645
646
647
648
649
650
651
652
653
654
655
656
657
658
659
660
661
662
663
664
665
666
667
668
669
670
671
672

673
674
675
676
677
678
679
680
681
682
683
684
685
686
687
688
689
690
691
692
693
694
695
696
697
698
699
700
701
702
703
704
705
706
707
708
709
710
711
712
713
714
715
716
717
718
719
720

721
722
723
724
725
726
727
728
729
730
731
732
733
734
735
736
737
738
739
740
741
742
743
744
745
746
747
748
749
750
751
752
753
754
755
756
757
758
759
760
761
762
763
764
765
766
767
768

769
770
771
772
773
774
775
776
777
778
779
780
781
782
783
784
785
786
787
788
789
790
791
792
793
794
795
796
797
798
799
800
801
802
803
804
805
806
807
808
809
810
811
812
813
814
815
816

817
818
819
820
821
822
823
824
825
826
827
828
829
830
831
832
833
834
835
836
837
838
839
840
841
842
843
844
845
846
847
848
849
850
851
852
853
854
855
856
857
858
859
860
861
862
863
864

865
866
867
868
869
870
871
872
873
874
875
876
877
878
879
880
881
882
883
884
885
886
887
888
889
890
891
892
893
894
895
896
897
898
899
900
901
902
903
904
905
906
907
908
909
910
911
912

The rhythms on this page are on **track 20** of the audio file

The rhythms on this page are on **track 21** of the audio file

The rhythms on this page are on **track 22** of the audio file

1057
1058
1059
1060
1061
1062
1063
1064
1065
1066
1067
1068
1069
1070
1071
1072
1073
1074
1075
1076
1077
1078
1079
1080
1081
1082
1083
1084
1085
1086
1087
1088
1089
1090
1091
1092
1093
1094
1095
1096
1097
1098
1099
1100
1101
1102
1103
1104

The rhythms on this page are on **track 24** of the audio file

1153 1154 1155 1156
1157 1158 1159 1160
1161 1162 1163 1164
1165 1166 1167 1168
1169 1170 1171 1172
1173 1174 1175 1176
1177 1178 1179 1180
1181 1182 1183 1184
1185 1186 1187 1188
1189 1190 1191 1192
1193 1194 1195 1196
1197 1198 1199 1200

1201 1202 1203 1204
1205 1206 1207 1208
1209 1210 1211 1212
1213 1214 1215 1216
1217 1218 1219 1220
1221 1222 1223 1224
1225 1226 1227 1228
1229 1230 1231 1232
1233 1234 1235 1236
1237 1238 1239 1240
1241 1242 1243 1244
1245 1246 1247 1248

1249
1250
1251
1252
1253
1254
1255
1256
1257
1258
1259
1260
1261
1262
1263
1264
1265
1266
1267
1268
1269
1270
1271
1272
1273
1274
1275
1276
1277
1278
1279
1280
1281
1282
1283
1284
1285
1286
1287
1288
1289
1290
1291
1292
1293
1294
1295
1296

The rhythms on this page are on **track 28** of the audio file

1345
1346
1347
1348
1349
1350
1351
1352
1353
1354
1355
1356
1357
1358
1359
1360
1361
1362
1363
1364
1365
1366
1367
1368
1369
1370
1371
1372
1373
1374
1375
1376
1377
1378
1379
1380
1381
1382
1383
1384
1385
1386
1387
1388
1389
1390
1391
1392

The rhythms on this page are on **track 30** of the audio file

1441
1442
1443
1444
1445
1446
1447
1448
1449
1450
1451
1452
1453
1454
1455
1456
1457
1458
1459
1460
1461
1462
1463
1464
1465
1466
1467
1468
1469
1470
1471
1472
1473
1474
1475
1476
1477
1478
1479
1480
1481
1482
1483
1484
1485
1486
1487
1488

The rhythms on this page are on **track 32** of the audio file

1537
1538
1539
1540
1541
1542
1543
1544
1545
1546
1547
1548
1549
1550
1551
1552
1553
1554
1555
1556
1557
1558
1559
1560
1561
1562
1563
1564
1565
1566
1567
1568
1569
1570
1571
1572
1573
1574
1575
1576
1577
1578
1579
1580
1581
1582
1583
1584

The rhythms on this page are on **track 34** of the audio file

The rhythms on this page are on **track 35** of the audio file

The rhythms on this page are on **track 36** of the audio file

1729
1730
1731
1732
1733
1734
1735
1736
1737
1738
1739
1740
1741
1742
1743
1744
1745
1746
1747
1748
1749
1750
1751
1752
1753
1754
1755
1756
1757
1758
1759
1760
1761
1762
1763
1764
1765
1766
1767
1768
1769
1770
1771
1772
1773
1774
1775
1776

The rhythms on this page are on **track 38** of the audio file

1825
1826
1827
1828
1829
1830
1831
1832
1833
1834
1835
1836
1837
1838
1839
1840
1841
1842
1843
1844
1845
1846
1847
1848
1849
1850
1851
1852
1853
1854
1855
1856
1857
1858
1859
1860
1861
1862
1863
1864
1865
1866
1867
1868
1869
1870
1871
1872

1873
1874
1875
1876
1877
1878
1879
1880
1881
1882
1883
1884
1885
1886
1887
1888
1889
1890
1891
1892
1893
1894
1895
1896
1897
1898
1899
1900
1901
1902
1903
1904
1905
1906
1907
1908
1909
1910
1911
1912
1913
1914
1915
1916
1917
1918
1919
1920

1921 1922 1923 1924
1925 1926 1927 1928
1929 1930 1931 1932
1933 1934 1935 1936
1937 1938 1939 1940
1941 1942 1943 1944
1945 1946 1947 1948
1949 1950 1951 1952
1953 1954 1955 1956
1957 1958 1959 1960
1961 1962 1963 1964
1965 1966 1967 1968

The rhythms on this page are on **track 42** of the audio file

2017
2018
2019
2020
2021
2022
2023
2024
2025
2026
2027
2028
2029
2030
2031
2032
2033
2034
2035
2036
2037
2038
2039
2040
2041
2042
2043
2044
2045
2046
2047
2048
2049
2050
2051
2052
2053
2054
2055
2056
2057
2058
2059
2060
2061
2062
2063
2064

The rhythms on this page are on **track 44** of the audio file

2113
2114
2115
2116
2117
2118
2119
2120
2121
2122
2123
2124
2125
2126
2127
2128
2129
2130
2131
2132
2133
2134
2135
2136
2137
2138
2139
2140
2141
2142
2143
2144
2145
2146
2147
2148
2149
2150
2151
2152
2153
2154
2155
2156
2157
2158
2159
2160

The rhythms on this page are on **track 46** of the audio file

2209
2210
2211
2212
2213
2214
2215
2216
2217
2218
2219
2220
2221
2222
2223
2224
2225
2226
2227
2228
2229
2230
2231
2232
2233
2234
2235
2236
2237
2238
2239
2240
2241
2242
2243
2244
2245
2246
2247
2248
2249
2250
2251
2252
2253
2254
2255
2256

The rhythms on this page are on **track 48** of the audio file

2305
2306
2307
2308
2309
2310
2311
2312
2313
2314
2315
2316
2317
2318
2319
2320
2321
2322
2323
2324
2325
2326
2327
2328
2329
2330
2331
2332
2333
2334
2335
2336
2337
2338
2339
2340
2341
2342
2343
2344
2345
2346
2347
2348
2349
2350
2351
2352

The rhythms on this page are on **track 50** of the audio file

2401
2402
2403
2404
2405
2406
2407
2408
2409
2410
2411
2412
2413
2414
2415
2416
2417
2418
2419
2420
2421
2422
2423
2424
2425
2426
2427
2428
2429
2430
2431
2432
2433
2434
2435
2436
2437
2438
2439
2440
2441
2442
2443
2444
2445
2446
2447
2448

The rhythms on this page are on **track 52** of the audio file

2497
2498
2499
2500
2501
2502
2503
2504
2505
2506
2507
2508
2509
2510
2511
2512
2513
2514
2515
2516
2517
2518
2519
2520
2521
2522
2523
2524
2525
2526
2527
2528
2529
2530
2531
2532
2533
2534
2535
2536
2537
2538
2539
2540
2541
2542
2543
2544

The rhythms on this page are on **track 54** of the audio file

2593
2594
2595
2596
2597
2598
2599
2600
2601
2602
2603
2604
2605
2606
2607
2608
2609
2610
2611
2612
2613
2614
2615
2616
2617
2618
2619
2620
2621
2622
2623
2624
2625
2626
2627
2628
2629
2630
2631
2632
2633
2634
2635
2636
2637
2638
2639
2640

2641
2642
2643
2644
2645
2646
2647
2648
2649
2650
2651
2652
2653
2654
2655
2656
2657
2658
2659
2660
2661
2662
2663
2664
2665
2666
2667
2668
2669
2670
2671
2672
2673
2674
2675
2676
2677
2678
2679
2680
2681
2682
2683
2684
2685
2686
2687
2688

2689
2690
2691
2692
2693
2694
2695
2696
2697
2698
2699
2700
2701
2702
2703
2704
2705
2706
2707
2708
2709
2710
2711
2712
2713
2714
2715
2716
2717
2718
2719
2720
2721
2722
2723
2724
2725
2726
2727
2728
2729
2730
2731
2732
2733
2734
2735
2736

2737
2738
2739
2740
2741
2742
2743
2744
2745
2746
2747
2748
2749
2750
2751
2752
2753
2754
2755
2756
2757
2758
2759
2760
2761
2762
2763
2764
2765
2766
2767
2768
2769
2770
2771
2772
2773
2774
2775
2776
2777
2778
2779
2780
2781
2782
2783
2784

2785
2786
2787
2788
2789
2790
2791
2792
2793
2794
2795
2796
2797
2798
2799
2800
2801
2802
2803
2804
2805
2806
2807
2808
2809
2810
2811
2812
2813
2814
2815
2816
2817
2818
2819
2820
2821
2822
2823
2824
2825
2926
2827
2828
2829
2830
2831
2832

The rhythms on this page are on **track 60** of the audio file

2881
2882
2883
2884
2885
2886
2887
2888
2889
2890
2891
2892
2893
2894
2895
2896
2897
2898
2899
2900
2901
2902
2903
2904
2905
2906
2907
2908
2909
2910
2911
2912
2913
2914
2915
2916
2917
2918
2919
2920
2921
2922
2923
2924
2925
2926
2927
2928

The rhythms on this page are on **track 62** of the audio file

2977
2978
2979
2980
2981
2982
2983
2984
2985
2986
2987
2988
2989
2990
2991
2992
2993
2994
2995
2996
2997
2998
2999
3000
3001
3002
3003
3004
3005
3006
3007
3008
3009
3010
3011
3012
3013
3014
3015
3016
3017
3018
3019
3020
3021
3022
3023
3024

The rhythms on this page are on **track 64** of the audio file

3073
3074
3075
3076
3077
3078
3079
3080
3081
3082
3083
3084
3085
3086
3087
3088
3089
3090
3091
3092
3093
3094
3095
3096
3097
3098
3099
3100
3101
3102
3103
3104
3105
3106
3107
3108
3109
3110
3111
3112
3113
3114
3115
3116
3117
3118
3119
3120

3121
3122
3123
3124
3125
3126
3127
3128
3129
3130
3131
3132
3133
3134
3135
3136
3137
3138
3139
3140
3141
3142
3143
3144
3145
3146
3147
3148
3149
3150
3151
3152
3153
3154
3155
3156
3157
3158
3159
3160
3161
3162
3163
3164
3165
3166
3167
3168

3169
3170
3171
3172
3173
3174
3175
3176
3177
3178
3179
3180
3181
3182
3183
3184
3185
3186
3187
3188
3189
3190
3191
3192
3193
3194
3195
3196
3197
3198
3199
3200
3201
3202
3203
3204
3205
3206
3207
3208
3209
3210
3211
3212
3213
3214
3215
3216

3217
3218
3219
3220
3221
3222
3223
3224
3225
3226
3227
3228
3229
3230
3231
3232
3233
3234
3235
3236
3237
3238
3239
3240
3241
3242
3243
3244
3245
3246
3247
3248
3249
3250
3251
3252
3253
3254
3255
3256
3257
3258
3259
3260
3261
3262
3263
3264

3265
3266
3267
3268
3269
3270
3271
3272
3273
3274
3275
3276
3277
3278
3279
3280
3281
3282
3283
3284
3285
3286
3287
3288
3289
3290
3291
3292
3293
3294
3295
3296
3297
3298
3299
3300
3301
3302
3303
3304
3305
3306
3307
3308
3309
3310
3311
3312

The rhythms on this page are on **track 70** of the audio file

3361
3362
3363
3364
3365
3366
3367
3368
3369
3370
3371
3372
3373
3374
3375
3376
3377
3378
3379
3380
3381
3382
3383
3384
3385
3386
3387
3388
3389
3390
3391
3392
3393
3394
3395
3396
3397
3398
3399
3400
3401
3402
3403
3404
3405
3406
3407
3408

3409
3410
3411
3412
3413
3414
3415
3416
3417
3418
3419
3420
3421
3422
3423
3424
3425
3426
3427
3428
3429
3430
3431
3432
3433
3434
3435
3436
3437
3438
3439
3440
3441
3442
3443
3444
3445
3446
3447
3448
3449
3450
3451
3452
3453
3454
3455
3456

3457
3458
3459
3460
3461
3462
3463
3464
3465
3466
3467
3468
3469
3470
3471
3472
3473
3474
3475
3476
3477
3478
3479
3480
3481
3482
3483
3484
3485
3486
3487
3488
3489
3490
3491
3492
3493
3494
3495
3496
3497
3498
3499
3500
3501
3502
3503
3504

3505
3506
3507
3508
3509
3510
3511
3512
3513
3514
3515
3516
3517
3518
3519
3520
3521
3522
3523
3524
3525
3526
3527
3528
3529
3530
3531
3532
3533
3534
3535
3536
3537
3538
3539
3540
3541
3542
3543
3544
3545
3546
3547
3548
3549
3550
3551
3552

3553
3554
3555
3556
3557
3558
3559
3560
3561
3562
3563
3564
3565
3566
3567
3568
3569
3570
3571
3572
3573
3574
3575
3576
3577
3578
3579
3580
3581
3582
3583
3584
3585
3586
3587
3588
3589
3590
3591
3592
3593
3594
3595
3596
3597
3598
3599
3600

3601
3602
3603
3604
3605
3606
3607
3608
3609
3610
3611
3612
3613
3614
3615
3616
3617
3618
3619
3620
3621
3622
3623
3624
3625
3626
3627
3628
3629
3630
3631
3632
3633
3634
3635
3636
3637
3638
3639
3640
3641
3642
3643
3644
3645
3646
3647
3648

3649 3650 3651 3652
3653 3654 3655 3656
3657 3658 3659 3660
3661 3662 3663 3664
3665 3666 3667 3668
3669 3670 3671 3672
3673 3674 3675 3676
3677 3678 3679 3680
3681 3682 3683 3684
3685 3686 3687 3688
3689 3690 3691 3692
3693 3694 3695 3696

The rhythms on this page are on **track 78** of the audio file

3745 3746 3747 3748
3749 3750 3751 3752
3753 3754 3755 3756
3757 3758 3759 3760
3761 3762 3763 3764
3765 3766 3767 3768
3769 3770 3771 3772
3773 3774 3775 3776
3777 3778 3779 3780
3781 3782 3783 3784
3785 3786 3787 3788
3789 3790 3791 3792

The rhythms on this page are on **track 80** of the audio file

3841
3842
3843
3844
3845
3846
3847
3848
3849
3850
3851
3852
3853
3854
3855
3856
3857
3858
3859
3860
3861
3862
3863
3864
3865
3866
3867
3868
3869
3870
3871
3872
3873
3874
3875
3876
3877
3878
3879
3880
3881
3882
3883
3884
3885
3886
3887
3888

3889
3890
3891
3892
3893
3894
3895
3986
3897
3898
3899
3900
3901
3902
3903
3904
3905
3906
3907
3908
3909
3910
3911
3912
3913
3914
3915
3916
3917
3918
3919
3920
3921
3922
3923
3924
3925
3926
3927
3928
3929
3930
3931
3932
3933
3934
3935
3936

3937
3938
3939
3940
3941
3942
3943
3944
3945
3946
3947
3948
3949
3950
3951
3952
3953
3954
3955
3956
3957
3958
3959
3960
3961
3962
3963
3964
3965
3966
3967
3968
3969
3970
3971
3972
3973
3974
3975
3976
3977
3978
3979
3980
3981
3982
3983
3984

The rhythms on this page are on **track 84** of the audio file

4033
4034
4035
4036
4037
4038
4039
4040
4041
4042
4043
4044
4045
4046
4047
4048
4049
4050
4051
4052
4053
4054
4055
4056
4057
4058
4059
4060
4061
4062
4063
4064
4065
4066
4067
4068
4069
4070
4071
4072
4073
4074
4075
4076
4077
4078
4079
4080

The rhythms on this page are on **track 86** of the audio file

4129
4130
4131
4132
4133
4134
4135
4136
4137
4138
4139
4140
4141
4142
4143
4144
4145
4146
4147
4148
4149
4150
4151
4152
4153
4154
4155
4156
4157
4158
4159
4160
4161
4162
4163
4164
4165
4166
4167
4168
4169
4170
4171
4172
4173
4174
4175
4176

The rhythms on this page are on **track 88** of the audio file

4225
4226
4227
4228
4229
4230
4231
4232
4233
4234
4235
4236
4237
4238
4239
4240
4241
4242
4243
4244
4245
4246
4247
4248
4249
4250
4251
4252
4253
4254
4255
4256
4257
4258
4259
4260
4261
4262
4263
4264
4265
4266
4267
4268
4269
4270
4271
4272

4273
4274
4275
4276
4277
4278
4279
4280
4281
4282
4283
4284
4285
4286
4287
4288
4289
4290
4291
4292
4293
4294
4295
4296
4297
4298
4299
4300
4301
4302
4303
4304
4305
4306
4307
4308
4309
4310
4311
4312
4313
4314
4315
4316
4317
4318
4319
4320

4321
4322
4323
4324
4325
4326
4327
4328
4329
4330
4331
4332
4333
4334
4335
4336
4337
4338
4339
4340
4341
4342
4343
4344
4345
4346
4347
4348
4349
4350
4351
4352
4353
4354
4355
4356
4357
4358
4359
4360
4361
4362
4363
4364
4365
4366
4367
4368

The rhythms on this page are on **track 92** of the audio file

4417
4418
4419
4420
4421
4422
4423
4424
4425
4426
4427
4428
4429
4430
4431
4432
4433
4434
4435
4436
4437
4438
4439
4440
4441
4442
4443
4444
4445
4446
4447
4448
4449
4450
4451
4452
4453
4454
4455
4456
4457
4458
4459
4460
4461
4462
4463
4464

The rhythms on this page are on **track 94** of the audio file

4513
4514
4515
4516
4517
4518
4519
4520
4521
4522
4523
4524
4525
4526
4527
4528
4529
4530
4531
4532
4533
4534
4535
4536
4537
4538
4539
4540
4541
4542
4543
4544
4545
4546
4547
4548
4549
4550
4551
4552
4553
4554
4555
4556
4557
4558
4559
4560

4561
4562
4563
4564
4565
4566
4567
4568
4569
4570
4571
4572
4573
4574
4575
4576
4577
4578
4579
4580
4581
4582
4583
4584
4585
4586
4587
4588
4589
4590
4591
4592
4593
4594
4595
4596
4597
4598
4599
4600
4601
4602
4603
4604
4605
4606
4607
4608

4609
4610
4611
4612
4613
4614
4615
4616
4617
4618
4619
4620
4621
4622
4623
4624
4625
4626
4627
4628
4629
4630
4631
4632
4633
4634
4635
4636
4637
4638
4639
4640
4641
4642
4643
4644
4645
4646
4647
4648
4649
4650
4651
4652
4653
4654
4655
4656

The rhythms on this page are on **track 98** of the audio file

4705
4706
4707
4708
4709
4710
4711
4712
4713
4714
4715
4716
4717
4718
4719
4720
4721
4722
4723
4724
4725
4726
4727
4728
4729
4730
4731
4732
4733
4734
4735
4736
4737
4738
4739
4740
4741
4742
4743
4744
4745
4746
4747
4748
4749
4750
4751
4752

The rhythms on this page are on **track 100** of the audio file

4801
4802
4803
4804
4805
4806
4807
4808
4809
4810
4811
4812
4813
4814
4815
4816
4817
4818
4819
4820
4821
4822
4823
4824
4825
4826
4827
4828
4829
4830
4831
4832
4833
4834
4835
4836
4837
4838
4839
4840
4841
4842
4843
4844
4845
4846
4847
4848

The rhythms on this page are on **track 102** of the audio file

4897
4898
4899
4900
4901
4902
4903
4904
4905
4906
4907
4908
4909
4910
4911
4912
4913
4914
4915
4916
4917
4918
4919
4920
4921
4922
4923
4924
4925
4926
4927
4928
4929
4930
4931
4932
4933
4934
4935
4936
4937
4938
4939
4940
4941
4942
4943
4944

4945
4946
4947
4948
4949
4950
4951
4952
4953
4954
4955
4956
4957
4958
4959
4960
4961
4962
4963
4964
4965
4966
4967
4968
4969
4970
4971
4972
4973
4974
4975
4976
4977
4978
4979
4980
4981
4982
4983
4984
4985
4986
4987
4988
4989
4990
4991
4992

The rhythms on this page are on **track 105** of the audio file

The rhythms on this page are on **track 106** of the audio file

5089
5090
5091
5092
5093
5094
5095
5096
5097
5098
5099
5100
5101
5102
5103
5104
5105
5106
5107
5108
5109
5110
5111
5112
5113
5114
5115
5116
5117
5118
5119
5120
5121
5122
5123
5124
5125
5126
5127
5128
5129
5130
5131
5132
5133
5134
5135
5136

5137 5138 5139 5140
5141 5142 5143 5144
5145 5146 5147 5148
5149 5150 5151 5152
5153 5154 5155 5156
5157 5158 5159 5160
5161 5162 5163 5164
5165 5166 5167 5168
5169 5170 5171 5172
5173 5174 5175 5176
5177 5178 5179 5180
5181 5182 5183 5184

5185
5186
5187
5188
5189
5190
5191
5192
5193
5194
5195
5196
5197
5198
5199
5200
5201
5202
5203
5204
5205
5206
5207
5208
5209
5210
5211
5212
5213
5214
5215
5216
5217
5218
5219
5220
5221
5222
5223
5224
5225
5226
5227
5228
5229
5230
5231
5232

The rhythms on this page are on **track 110** of the audio file

5281
5282
5283
5284
5285
5286
5287
5288
5289
5290
5291
5292
5293
5294
5295
5296
5297
5298
5299
5300
5301
5302
5303
5304
5305
5306
5307
5308
5309
5310
5311
5312
5313
5314
5315
5316
5317
5318
5319
5320
5321
5322
5323
5324
5325
5326
5327
5328

5329
5330
5331
5332
5333
5334
5335
5336
5337
5338
5339
5340
5341
5342
5343
5344
5345
5346
5347
5348
5349
5350
5351
5352
5353
5354
5355
5356
5357
5358
5359
5360
5361
5362
5363
5364
5365
5366
5367
5368
5369
5370
5371
5372
5373
5374
5375
5376

5377
5378
5379
5380
5381
5382
5383
5384
5385
5386
5387
5388
5389
5390
5391
5392
5393
5394
5395
5396
5397
5398
5399
5400
5401
5402
5403
5404
5405
5406
5407
5408
5409
5410
5411
5412
5413
5414
5415
5416
5417
5418
5419
5420
5421
5422
5423
5424

5425
5426
5427
5428
5429
5430
5431
5432
5433
5434
5435
5436
5437
5438
5439
5440
5441
5442
5443
5444
5445
5446
5447
5448
5449
5450
5451
5452
5453
5454
5455
5456
5457
5458
5459
5460
5461
5462
5463
5464
5465
5466
5467
5468
5469
5470
5471
5472

5473 5474 5475 5476
5477 5478 5479 5480
5481 5482 5483 5484
5485 5486 5487 5488
5489 5490 5491 5492
5493 5494 5495 5496
5497 5498 5499 5500
5501 5502 5503 5504
5505 5506 5507 5508
5509 5510 5511 5512
5513 5514 5515 5516
5517 5518 5519 5520

5521
5522
5523
5524
5525
5526
5527
5528
5529
5530
5531
5532
5533
5534
5535
5536
5537
5538
5539
5540
5541
5542
5543
5544
5545
5546
5547
5548
5549
5550
5551
5552
5553
5554
5555
5556
5557
5558
5559
5560
5561
5562
5563
5564
5565
5566
5567
5568

5569
5570
5571
5572
5573
5574
5575
5576
5577
5578
5579
5580
5581
5582
5583
5584
5585
5586
5587
5588
5589
5590
5591
5592
5593
5594
5595
5596
5597
5598
5599
5600
5601
5602
5603
5604
5605
5606
5607
5608
5609
5610
5611
5612
5613
5614
5615
5616

5617
5618
5619
5620
5621
5622
5623
5624
5625
5626
5627
5628
5629
5630
5631
5632
5633
5634
5635
5636
5637
5638
5639
5640
5641
5642
5643
5644
5645
5646
5647
5648
5649
5650
5651
5652
5653
5654
5655
5656
5657
5658
5659
5660
5661
5662
5663
5664

5665
5666
5667
5668
5669
5670
5671
5672
5673
5674
5675
5676
5677
5678
5679
5680
5681
5682
5683
5684
5685
5686
5687
5688
5689
5690
5691
5692
5693
5694
5695
5696
5697
5698
5699
5700
5701
5702
5703
5704
5705
5706
5707
5708
5709
5710
5711
5712

5713
5714
5715
5716
5717
5718
5719
5720
5721
5722
5723
5724
5725
5726
5727
5728
5729
5730
5731
5732
5733
5734
5735
5736
5737
5738
5739
5740
5741
5742
5743
5744
5745
5746
5747
5748
5749
5750
5751
5752
5753
5754
5755
5756
5757
5758
5759
5760

5761
5762
5763
5764
5765
5766
5767
5768
5769
5770
5771
5772
5773
5774
5775
5776
5777
5778
5779
5780
5781
5782
5783
5784
5785
5786
5787
5788
5789
5790
5791
5792
5793
5794
5795
5796
5797
5798
5799
5800
5801
5802
5803
5804
5805
5806
5807
5808

5809
5810
5811
5812
5813
5814
5815
5816
5817
5818
5819
5820
5821
5822
5823
5824
5825
5826
5827
5828
5829
5830
5831
5832
5833
5834
5835
5836
5837
5838
5839
5840
5841
5842
5843
5844
5845
5846
5847
5848
5849
5850
5851
5852
5853
5854
5855
5856

5857
5858
5859
5860
5861
5862
5863
5864
5865
5866
5867
5868
5869
5870
5871
5872
5873
5874
5875
5876
5877
5878
5879
5880
5881
5882
5883
5884
5885
5886
5887
5888
5889
5890
5891
5892
5893
5894
5895
5896
5897
5898
5899
5900
5901
5902
5903
5904

 The rhythms on this page are on **track 124** of the audio file

5953
5954
5955
5956
5957
5958
5959
5960
5961
5962
5963
5964
5965
5966
5967
5968
5969
5970
5971
5972
5973
5974
5975
5976
5977
5978
5979
5980
5981
5982
5983
5984
5985
5986
5987
5988
5989
5990
5991
5992
5993
5994
5995
5996
5997
5998
5999
6000

6001
6002
6003
6004
6005
6006
6007
6008
6009
6010
6011
6012
6013
6014
6015
6016
6017
6018
6019
6020
6021
6022
6023
6024
6025
6026
6027
6028
6029
6030
6031
6032
6033
6034
6035
6036
6037
6038
6039
6040
6041
6042
6043
6044
6045
6046
6047
6048

6049
6050
6051
6052
6053
6054
6055
6056
6057
6058
6059
6060
6061
6062
6063
6064
6065
6066
6067
6068
6069
6070
6071
6072
6073
6074
6075
6076
6077
6078
6079
6080
6081
6082
6083
6084
6085
6086
6087
6088
6089
6090
6091
6092
6093
6094
6095
6096

The rhythms on this page are on **track 128** of the audio file

6145
6146
6147
6148
6149
6150
6151
6152
6153
6154
6155
6156
6157
6158
6159
6160
6161
6162
6163
6164
6165
6166
6167
6168
6169
6170
6171
6172
6173
6174
6175
6176
6177
6178
6179
6180
6181
6182
6183
6184
6185
6186
6187
6188
6189
6190
6191
6192

The rhythms on this page are on **track 130** of the audio file

6241
6242
6243
6244
6245
6246
6247
6248
6249
6250
6251
6252
6253
6254
6255
6256
6257
6258
6259
6260
6261
6262
6263
6264
6265
6266
6267
6268
6269
6270
6271
6272
6273
6274
6275
6276
6277
6278
6279
6280
6281
6282
6283
6284
6285
6286
6287
6288

The rhythms on this page are on **track 132** of the audio file

6337
6338
6339
6340
6341
6342
6343
6344
6345
6346
6347
6348
6349
6350
6351
6352
6353
6354
6355
6356
6357
6358
6359
6360
6361
6362
6363
6364
6365
6366
6367
6368
6369
6370
6371
6372
6373
6374
6375
6376
6377
6378
6379
6380
6381
6382
6383
6384

The rhythms on this page are on **track 134** of the audio file

6433
6434
6435
6436
6437
6438
6439
6440
6441
6442
6443
6444
6445
6446
6447
6448
6449
6450
6451
6452
6453
6454
6455
6456
6457
6458
6459
6460
6461
6462
6463
6464
6465
6466
6467
6468
6469
6470
6471
6472
6473
6474
6475
6476
6477
6478
6479
6480

6481
6482
6483
6484
6485
6486
6487
6488
6489
6490
6491
6492
6493
6494
6495
6496
6497
6498
6499
6500
6501
6502
6503
6504
6505
6506
6507
6508
6509
6510
6511
6512
6513
6514
6515
6516
6517
6518
6519
6520
6521
6522
6523
6524
6525
6526
6527
6528

6529
6530
6531
6532
6533
6534
6535
6536
6537
6538
6539
6540
6541
6542
6543
6544
6545
6546
6547
6548
6549
6550
6551
6552
6553
6554
6555
6556
6557
6558
6559
6560
6561

Audio File Information

If you download the audio file for this book using the URL on the title page, you need to know how the audio file is organized so you can use it effectively. Each track of the audio file represents one page of rhythms from the book, and there is a note at the top of each page of the book telling which track contains the rhythms for that page.

Each rhythm is played through 4 times.

Pick a page in the book and go to the audio track with the rhythms for that page. When you play the audio track, you will hear the first rhythm on that page played through 4 times followed by about a two second pause, the second rhythm on that page played through 4 times followed by a pause, etc., until all of the rhythms on that page have been played.

The rhythms in the audio file are midi files and don't sound that much like real drums, but they will give you an idea of what the rhythms should sound like. The audio files are meant to simulate drum set playing.

The rhythms in the audio file are played at 132 beats per minute.

Daily Practice

I use the rhythms in this book for my daily conga practice. I play through each rhythm at least 4 times before moving on to the next rhythm. Since there are too many rhythms for me to play in one day, I make a note of where I stop so I can continue from there the next day.